The Sunsets of My Mind

———

a collection of poems

by
L D Stranack

l d stranack

"though my soul may set in darkness
it will rise in perfect flight,
i have loved the stars too fondly,
to be fearful of the night".

sarah williams~

---

the sunsets of my mind

l d stranack

she lived for sunsets.
and the sun died every night
surrendering in the hope of one
last chance to shine
upon her face.

/LS

the sunsets of my mind

l d stranack

in order to rise you have to fall.,
and in order to grow , you have to heal

the sunsets of my mind

l d stranack

yours are not the first
eyes i have mistaken
for home.
i have gazed upon
too many
that have promised
me solace.
but i can honestly say,
yours were by far
the hardest to
walk away from.

/LS

the sunsets of my mind

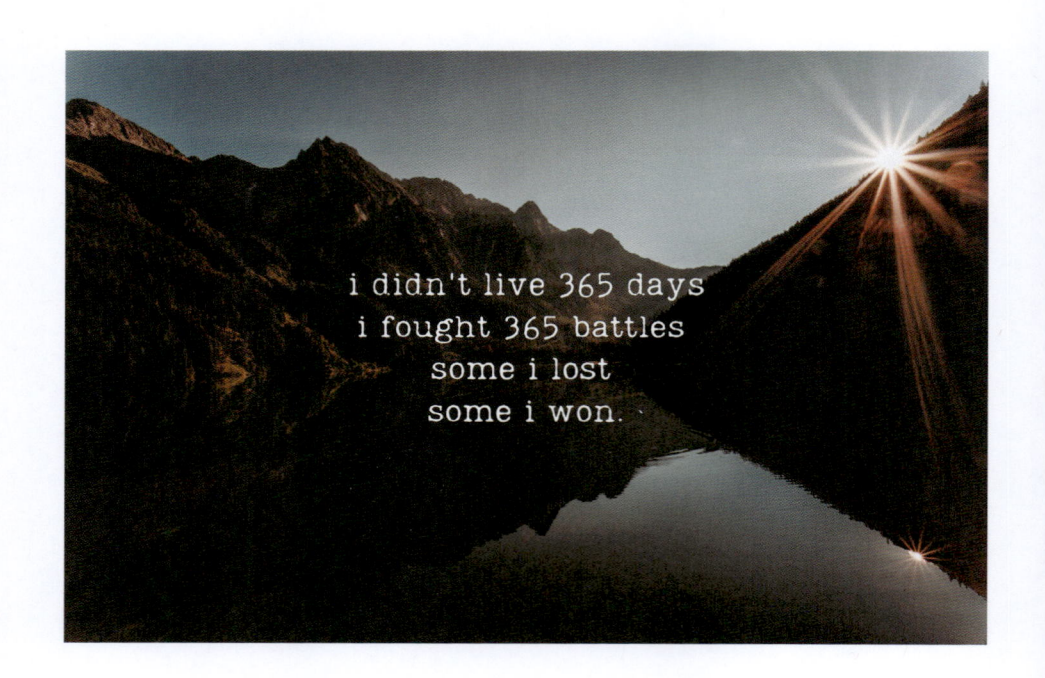

l d stranack

i didn't live 365 days
i fought 365 battles
some i lost
some i won.

the sunsets of my mind

l d stranack

i wasn't made for this world.
i am too sentient for the
brutality it yields.
i've never coped well with
anguish and suffering.
and even though i know
it is a part of human life,
it doesn't make the burden
any easier to bear.
my eyes have been witness to
too much wickedness,
my mind has been corrupted
by too many people,
my ears have been
betrayed with too many lies.
it's too harsh a place for me.

/LS

the sunsets of my mind

l d stranack

you were just a million lessons
disguised as a love story.

the sunsets of my mind

l d stranack

i've always held on longer
than i should have.
i didn't want to believe
i wasn't ever good enough.
and even though at times
i knew i was too good,
my fear caused
me to cling to
something that had to die
in the hope that i could
breathe new life into it
all endings are painful
when there is no life left to save.

/LS

the sunsets of my mind

l d stranack

"she smiled a a lot."
even when she was sad?
"especially when she
was sad".

the sunsets of my mind

l d stranack

don't tell me not to feel what i feel,
for my heart to betray itself.
you gave me the adoration
and the pain
and for that i love you
and despise you.
i was perfectly content in
my own bed of roses
until you came with your thorns,
so don't tell me i can't feel
my own heart bleeding when
you were the one who
cut me.

/LS

the sunsets of my mind

l d stranack

i'll meet you on that beach
in our next life.

the sunsets of my mind

l d stranack

when a relationship ends
where does all
the love go?
where do we store it?

/LS

the sunsets of my mind

l d stranack

you will always be my favourite hello
and my hardest goodbye

the sunsets of my mind

l d stranack

she looked at him like
he was the most perfect
thing she had
ever seen,
and he was, in her eyes.
he was perfection,
he didn't possess one flaw.
the world began
and ended with him.
she would never not love him,
no one else's smile would
completely melt her like his did.
she was putty in his hands.

/LS

the sunsets of my mind

l d stranack

the memories of you comfort me
even when your arms can't...

the sunsets of my mind

l d stranack

our love story is a poem
waiting to be read
by those love starved
souls wishing to be fed.

/LS

the sunsets of my mind

l d stranack

stay forever in my heart,
there is no other place you belong.

the sunsets of my mind

l d stranack

i don't know how it
is that i know you
so well,
i believe we have
danced in many
other lifetimes
with only the
stars above as onlookers.

/LS

the sunsets of my mind

l d stranack

perhaps one day, when we have the future
in our hands, might we delight
in the possibilities that await us.

the sunsets of my mind

l d stranack

i never did much planning,
i always just let things be.
and i've come to realise
that many things
will gravitate towards
you naturally,
if you attract them
with a calm loving
heart and a patient spirit.

/LS

the sunsets of my mind

l d stranack

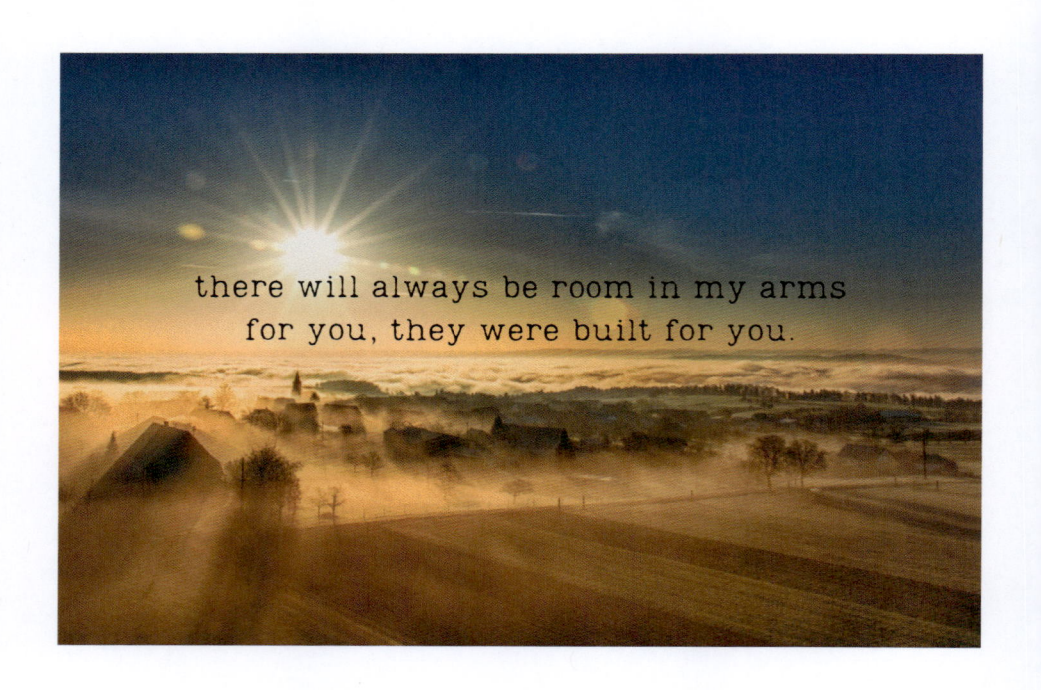

there will always be room in my arms
for you, they were built for you.

the sunsets of my mind

l d stranack

my body will age
and my heart
will grow weary,
and one day
i will cast off this
mortal frame
and be remembered
as the kind of woman
they named storms after.

/LS

the sunsets of my mind

l d stranack

my mind is filled with poems
about you that you will
never read.

the sunsets of my mind

l d stranack

i don't want the fire inside
of me put out.
the fire that you lit
that has burned my
heart countless times.
i need the embers to keep
my soul warm
otherwise i may perish and die,
like a plant without
the sun.

/LS

the sunsets of my mind

l d stranack

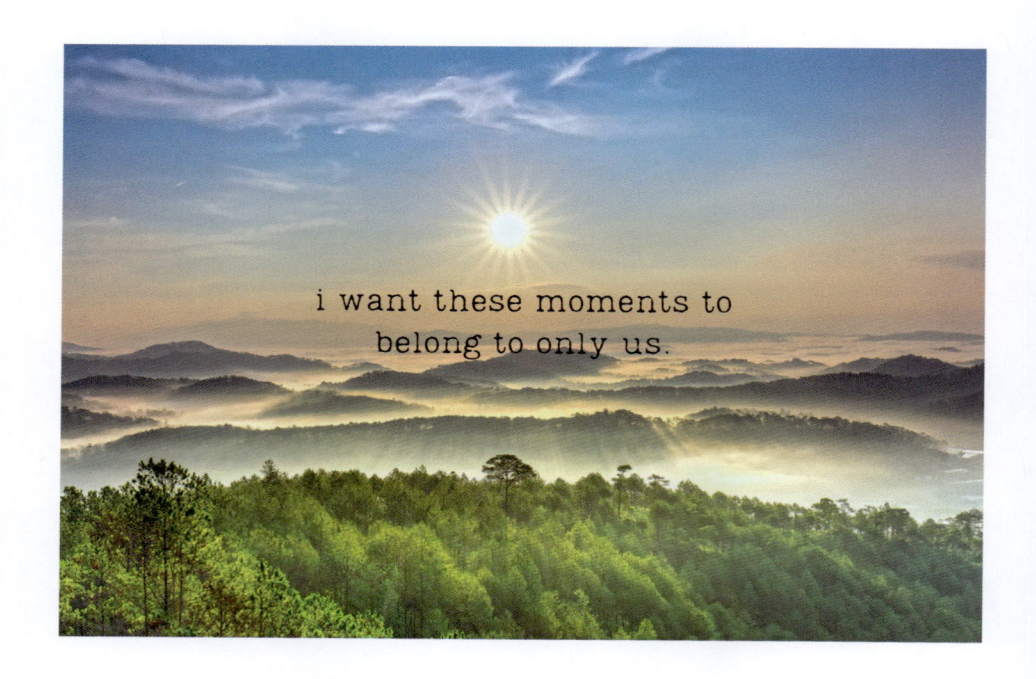

i want these moments to
belong to only us.

the sunsets of my mind

l d stranack

please, be kinder to yourself.
don't worry about being
too much or not enough,
let people show up for you ,
let people remind you how
extraordinary you are,
be vulnerable,
don't be afraid of what you feel.
connect with the moments
that bring tears to your eyes
and laughter to your cheeks.
embrace the uniqueness of yourself.
you are a wonder to behold
embrace every inch of yourself
and what you bring to
the world, and everything in it..
connect with it all
because beautiful things are
vanishing every single day.
don't let your own love
story be one of them.

/LS

the sunsets of my mind

l d stranack

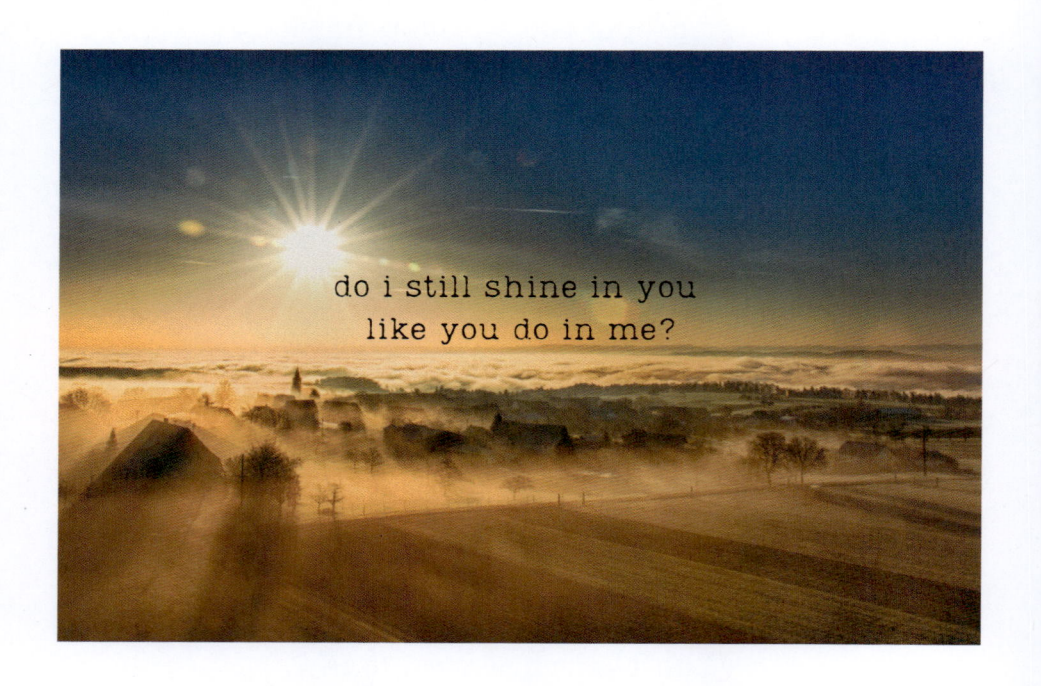

do i still shine in you
like you do in me?

the sunsets of my mind

l d stranack

i have no desire
to compete for love
if you have to choose
between me and another
choose them
if i was the one
you wouldn't hesitate.
i would consume every
atom of your body
and the thought of
being without me
should make your
heart fill with anguish
i will never be an option
i belong on a pedestal
of gold.

/LS

the sunsets of my mind

l d stranack

we will always be the book
with the last chapter torn out

the sunsets of my mind

l d stranack

don't look at me with that
pain behind your eyes
you may think you can
hide it but i know
what your soul looks like
from the inside
please don't suffer alone
let me help.
i can't take your pain away,
i so wish i could.
let me offer you my hand
to hold in troubled times,
i will share your burdens
with you.
don't think you're weak,
you're the strongest
person i know
and yet so pure and vulnerable.
just know that i
will never abandon you,
i will always be here for you.
you are a supernova in
a galaxy full of stars,
you light up my world.
i'd have lost my way
without you.

/LS

the sunsets of my mind

l d stranack

how brave you are to accept
what is and what will be.

the sunsets of my mind

l d stranack

poetry is where i feel
most like myself.
it has given me great
comfort and befriended me
when the loneliness
became too much.
it is my quiet escape
into the world of words,
the place i call home.

/LS

the sunsets of my mind

l d stranack

you and i will always
have unfinished business

the sunsets of my mind

l d stranack

open your eyes
to the magic that
is all around
let it come to you,
let it enthral you
and seep into your
bones
let it carry you
to the deepest realms
where anything is
possible
your heart's desires
are a mere whisper away.

/LS

the sunsets of my mind

l d stranack

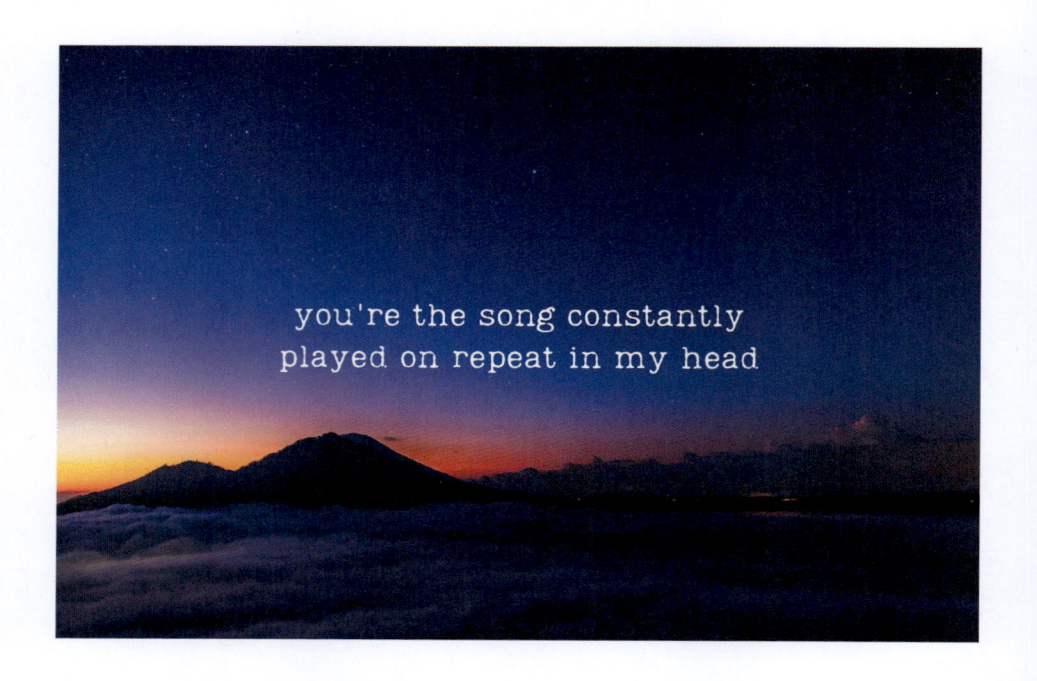

you're the song constantly
played on repeat in my head

the sunsets of my mind

l d stranack

listen more to your inner voice,
it is your dearest friend.
it lives inside you
watching and guiding silently.
your heart speaks to it
encouraging it to
volunteer its gifts.
so allow yourself moments
of peace to tune in.
let it hear your every wish,
and fulfil your destiny.
trust it more often,
it won't ever forsake you.

/LD

the sunsets of my mind

l d stranack

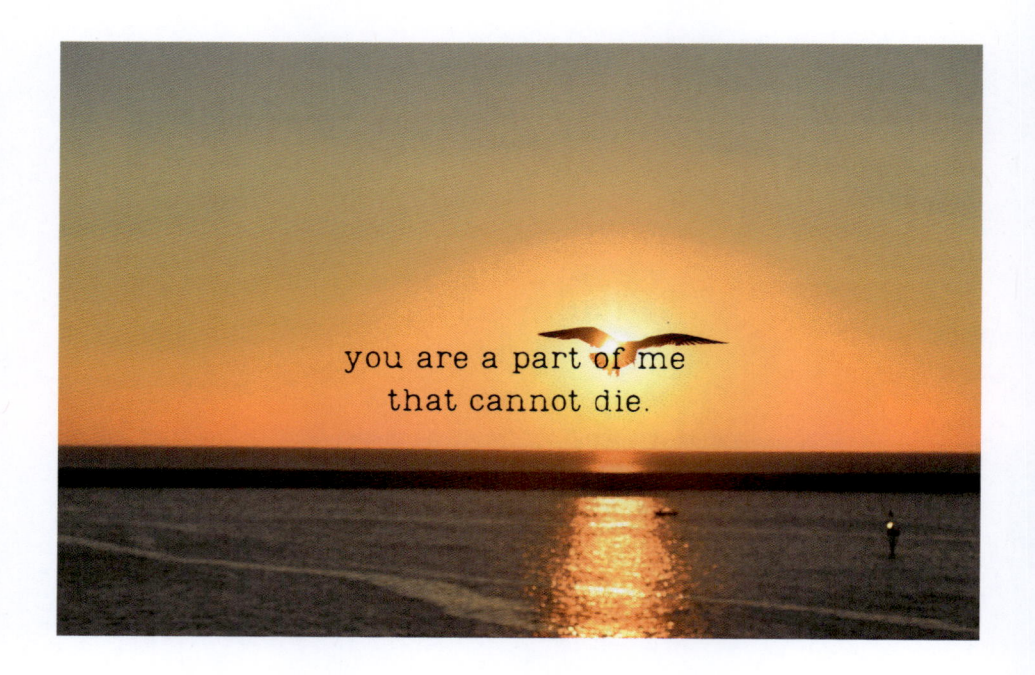

you are a part of me
that cannot die.

the sunsets of my mind

l d stranack

if i have given you my very all,
the best of what i have to give.
if i have loved you with
all that i am and sacrificed for you
and through any of that
if i have ever fallen short
in your eyes,
then maybe we are looking
for different things.

/LS

the sunsets of my mind

l d stranack

without the bad times you
could never appreciate the good

the sunsets of my mind

l d stranack

kiss me before you go.
hold my head in your hands
and taste the regret on my lips,
and as you walk away
i tell myself i don't need you anyway,
but my ego never was my friend.

/LS

the sunsets of my mind

l d stranack

you long to forget but your heart will always remember.

the sunsets of my mind

l d stranack

we all have a toxic habit of
focussing on other people's mistakes
most importantly our own.
we forget all the resilience we've gained
and the silent battles we've won.
it's a human trait , sabotaging.
instead, let's abstain and inspire
one another, in equal measures.

/LS

the sunsets of my mind

l d stranack

i wish i had all the words to
explain the emotions i feel every day

the sunsets of my mind

l d stranack

the secret of true happiness
is not found in pursuing more
but in developing the ability
to enjoy less.

/LS

the sunsets of my mind

l d stranack

stay soft when life becomes hard

the sunsets of my mind

l d stranack

the longing in his eyes
i finally bring my gaze to meet his,
my exaggerated breaths.
i attempt to slow down my breathing,
inhale, exhale
contract ,expand.
that sly grin as his fingers
wrap themselves around my face.
and he pulls me towards him.
my insides melt,
then the weight of his lips
are on mine.
and i must confess
i would die happily
in this moment.

/LS

the sunsets of my mind

l d stranack

a life of mediocrity is the waste of a life.

the sunsets of my mind

l d stranack

tears scar their way down my cheeks,
and a wave of jealousy
washes over me.
i have this ongoing battle
with my heart,
knowing that when he's
not with me he is with her.
and i know it is the price i pay
for loving someone
who was and never
will be mine.

/LS

the sunsets of my mind

l d stranack

art is an obsession some of us
don't want a cure for.

the sunsets of my mind

l d stranack

words can sometimes
have a far greater
effect on the heart
than a kiss.

/LS

the sunsets of my mind

l d stranack

i often put space between myself and others
when sadness rears its head.

the sunsets of my mind

l d stranack

she loved being in her own world
and she allowed him to be
a lucky observer.
and sometimes in those
silent moments together
with the absence of sound ,
he understood the things
she didn't even have to say.

/LS

the sunsets of my mind

l d stranack

he gave her something she
didn't even know she needed.

the sunsets of my mind

l d stranack

loving gestures,
causing me to soften,
to open up,
feeling my heart
getting fuller and fuller,
and as much as i
want it to be empty
It betrays me.yet again.

/LS

the sunsets of my mind

l d stranack

i'm too emotionally involved
in every single thing i do

the sunsets of my mind

l d stranack

the sadness in his voice
lashes out and scars my heart.
traces of tears form
in his eyes,
i yearn to just hold him
and wrap him in my arms,
embrace him and take his
fears away.
i love him so much,
i could write a thousand poems
about him and never
run out of words.

/LS

the sunsets of my mind

l d stranack

is life really that black and white?

the sunsets of my mind

l d stranack

sometimes in life ,
we need
a few bad days,
to put the good ones
into perspective.

/LS

the sunsets of my mind

l d stranack

my silence is an extension of
my wounded heart

the sunsets of my mind

l d stranack

what she's wishing she
could give him,
is something he never
even knew he needed.

/LS

the sunsets of my mind

l d stranack

self sabotage will always be the
nemesis of the perfectionist

the sunsets of my mind

l d stranack

create secrets with your heart,
share whispers no one
will ever hear.
for in the confines of
your heart
they will remain
safe and abstruse.
and trust that your heart
will never breathe a word
it is your dearest confidante.

/LS

the sunsets of my mind

l d stranack

like fireflies in the night,
her dreams linger in her mind

the sunsets of my mind

l d stranack

the love stories that fan the flames fastest
are the ones that are
extinguished the quickest.

/LS

the sunsets of my mind

l d stranack

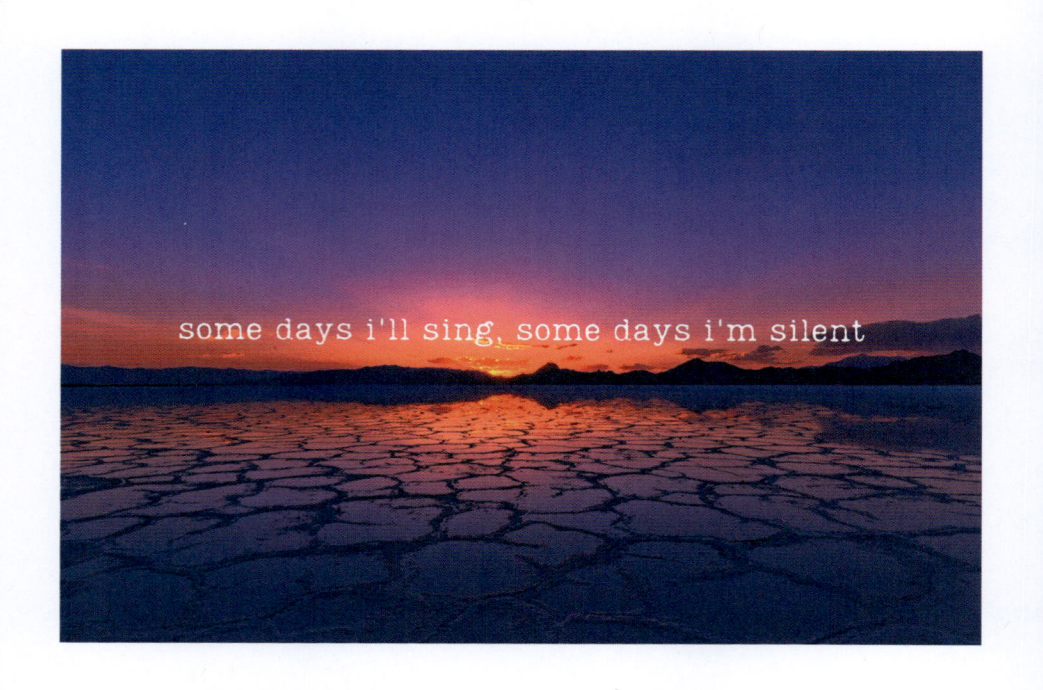

some days i'll sing, some days i'm silent

the sunsets of my mind

l d stranack

some people don't say
"i love you",
they say things like,
have you slept?
drive home safe,
i saw this and thought of you.
listen carefully, it's disguised
as concern.

/LS

the sunsets of my mind

l d stranack

people who sleep too much
spend half their life in their dreams

the sunsets of my mind

l d stranack

as she sat alone cross legged,
she pondered the reasons as
to why she was never meant
to be loved properly,
why she was always
in the middle of nowhere
when it came to matters
of the heart.
but she inherently knew
that she was too much
for most men,
and that gave her a sense
of contentment realising that
the middle of nowhere was
actually her comfort zone.

/LS

the sunsets of my mind

l d stranack

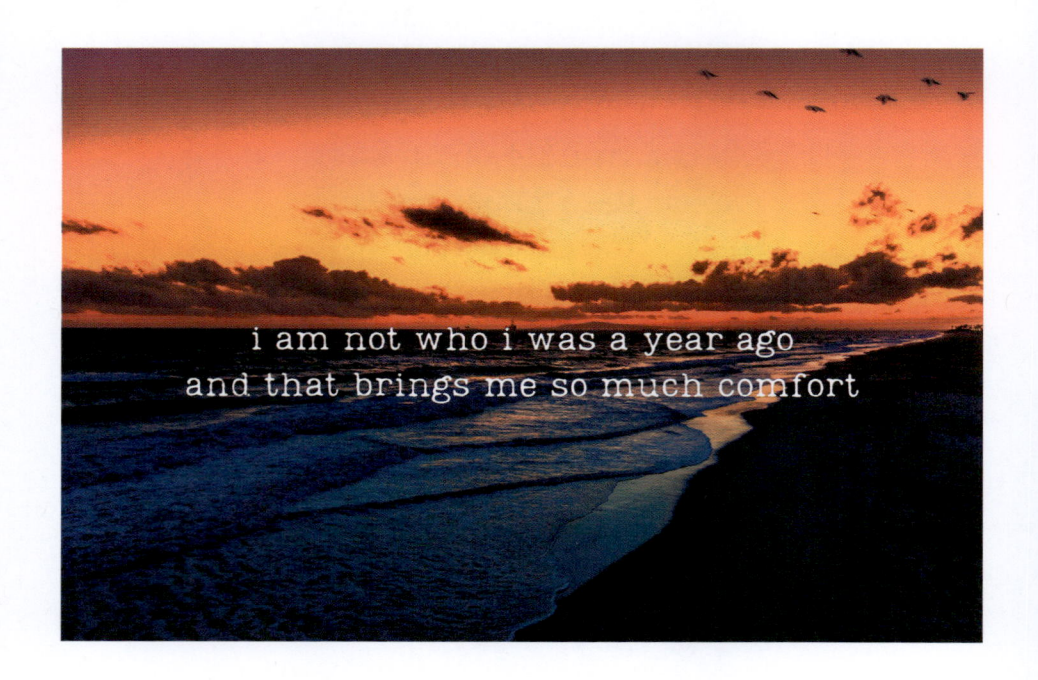

i am not who i was a year ago
and that brings me so much comfort

the sunsets of my mind

l d stranack

there's a yearning in my soul,
what it is i can't quite place,
but i know it's reminiscent
of a restlessness,
and i am looking out at the horizon
as far as it can go,
and all i know is
i might not see what's coming
but i'm ready.

/LS

the sunsets of my mind

l d stranack

don't tell me your fighting for me,
tell me you're outside my door begging to get in.

the sunsets of my mind

l d stranack

they say that home is where the heart is,
but if your heart isn't there,
is it really a home?

/LS

the sunsets of my mind

l d stranack

we all have a road we walk alone
but that doesn't make it desolate

the sunsets of my mind

l d stranack

how beautiful is it
to hear the love in someone's voice
when they speak your name.

/LS

the sunsets of my mind

l d stranack

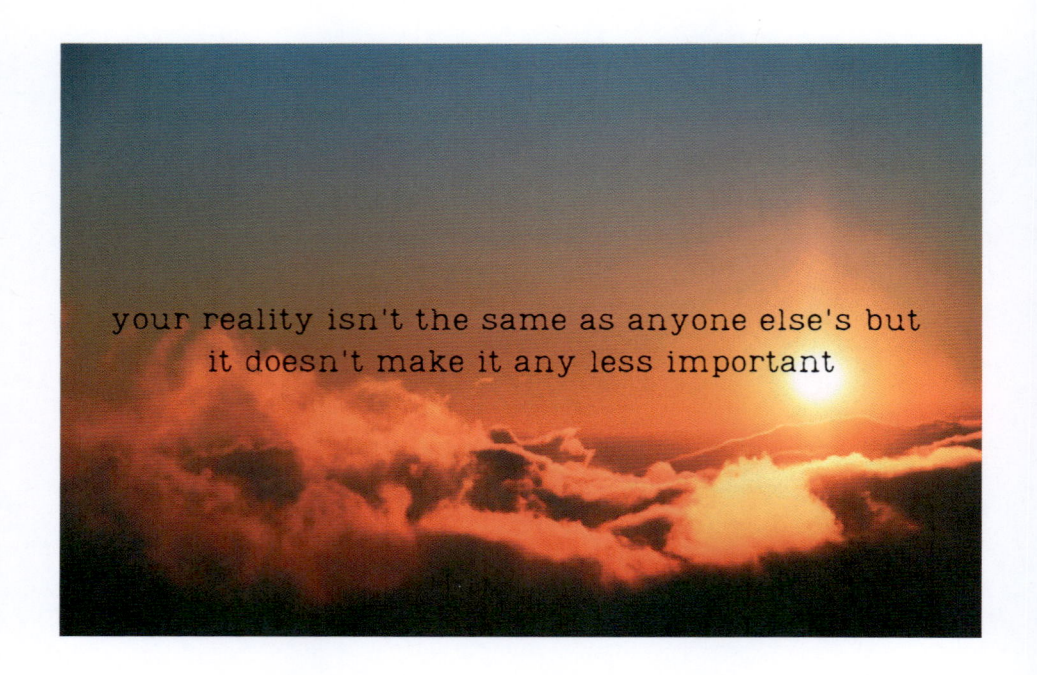

your reality isn't the same as anyone else's but it doesn't make it any less important

the sunsets of my mind

l d stranack

i am still learning how to
stop holding my breath
when waves of sadness
hit me.
i can't seem to keep my
head above water
and yet i cut off
my own air supply
wondering why i'm drowning.

/LS

the sunsets of my mind

l d stranack

countless apologies just lose their
authenticity over time

the sunsets of my mind

l d stranack

show me what it is to be human
and i'll show you the inhumanities
that come with it.
a huge dose of heroism is what
is needed for this life.

/LS

the sunsets of my mind

l d stranack

i think love is about finding people who bring
warmth to the coldness of life

the sunsets of my mind

l d stranack

i'm a very misunderstood person
by people who don't take the
time to get to know me properly,
and in their shortcomings
they fail to strip away the layers
i have accumulated that require patience
and love.
only pausing and focussing
on my so called flaws.
my flaws are the medals i adorn proudly,
for through gaining them they fail to see
the admirable qualities i possess
and the fearlessness on my part.
so if you can't recognise them,
you haven't earned .a place in my heart.
/LS

the sunsets of my mind

l d stranack

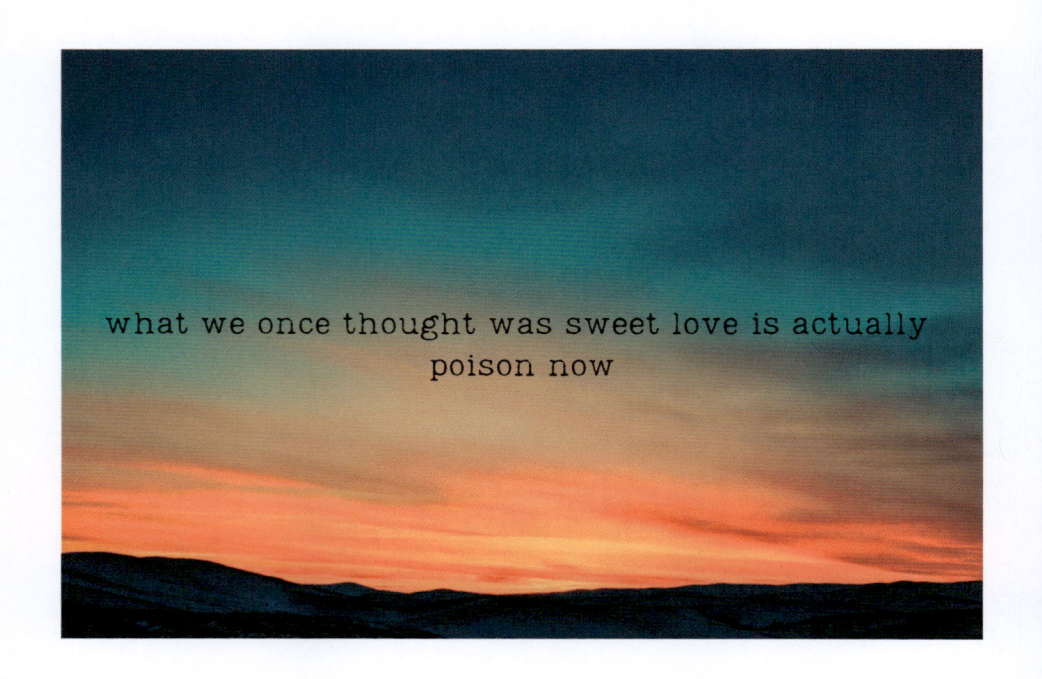

what we once thought was sweet love is actually poison now

the sunsets of my mind

l d stranack

imagine how boring our lives would be
if everything and everyone were perfect.
how dull and predictable things would be
if we could anticipate everything that
would happen
it is the randomness and the unknown
that mould us and the world
into something that has unpredictability
and in that unpredictability,
there is stimulus.
/LS

the sunsets of my mind

l d stranack

you can't change your past,
but you can change your past self

the sunsets of my mind

l d stranack

just because i have lost a petal or two
in the harsh winds of life
doesn't make my blossoms any
less beautiful.
i may be delicate and flimsy,
i am also sturdy, and resilient.
i will come into full bloom
again and again.

/LS

the sunsets of my mind

l d stranack

darling, this world isn't for us., let's go

the sunsets of my mind

l d stranack

sometimes your truth is too much
for some.
they see it as a form of attack.
i'm the gun ,my truth is the bullet,
i'll take aim and fire point blank.
and it may injure your ego,
and blow a hole in your denial,
but once that bullet penetrates,
you're going down
whether you like it or not.

/LS

the sunsets of my mind

l d stranack

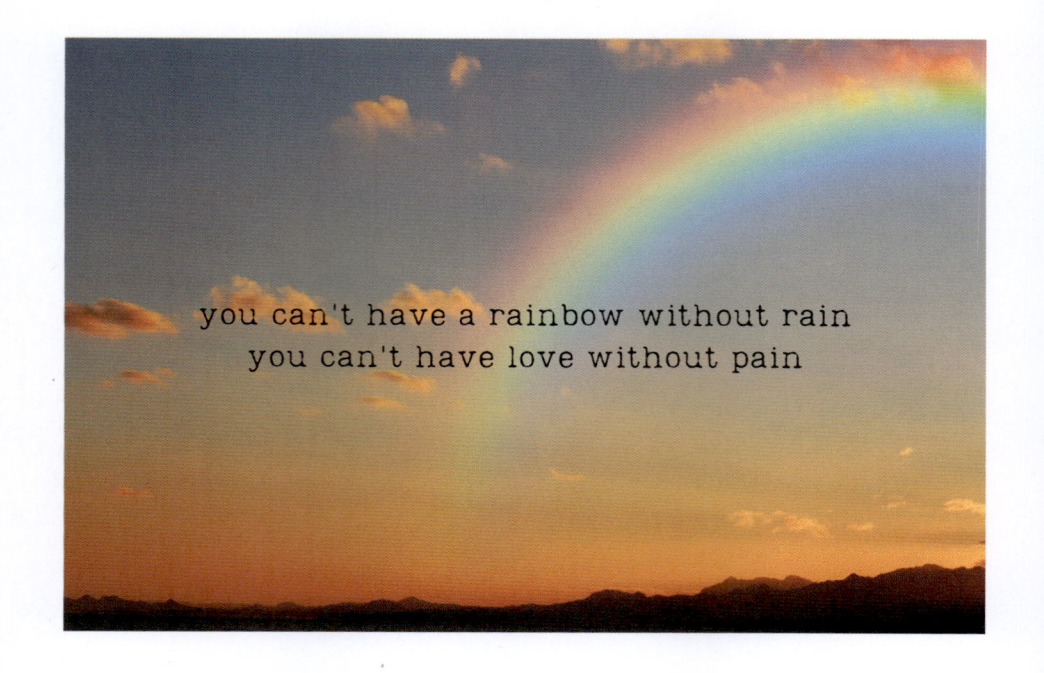

you can't have a rainbow without rain
you can't have love without pain

the sunsets of my mind

l d stranack

think before you hurt people.
they may say they forgive you
but they really won't forget,
and the seed of resentment will germinate
inside them
and sprout into injury.
so be careful what you sow
because the weeds of hurt
will grow.

/LS

the sunsets of my mind

l d stranack

if you're capable of blaming yourself for your brokenness
you're also capable of healing it

the sunsets of my mind

l d stranack

she feels everything so deeply
and brings warmth to the lives of those
she loves,
but sometimes there are days when
she wishes she could escape
from her own heart,
and run without looking back.

/LS

the sunsets of my mind

l d stranack

i'll never understand the negativity in others
but i wont waste my time trying

the sunsets of my mind

l d stranack

i give people way too many chances,
far more than they deserve.
and each time i hope they'll change,
they only prove me wrong.
and in proving me wrong they
taint the perception i have of myself
that somehow i'm not good enough,
that i'm an option they think
they can fall back on when
they need something.
and i openly give it because
inherently i'm a giver, a fixer.
but i'm done repairing egos
there will be no more chances.
you weren't even worth my weakness.

/LS

the sunsets of my mind

l d stranack

i'm stitching myself back together
but this time with different threads

the sunsets of my mind

l d stranack

i used your love like an umbrella
until i realised that you
were the storm.
and i don't take kindly
to being rained on.

/LS

the sunsets of my mind

l d stranack

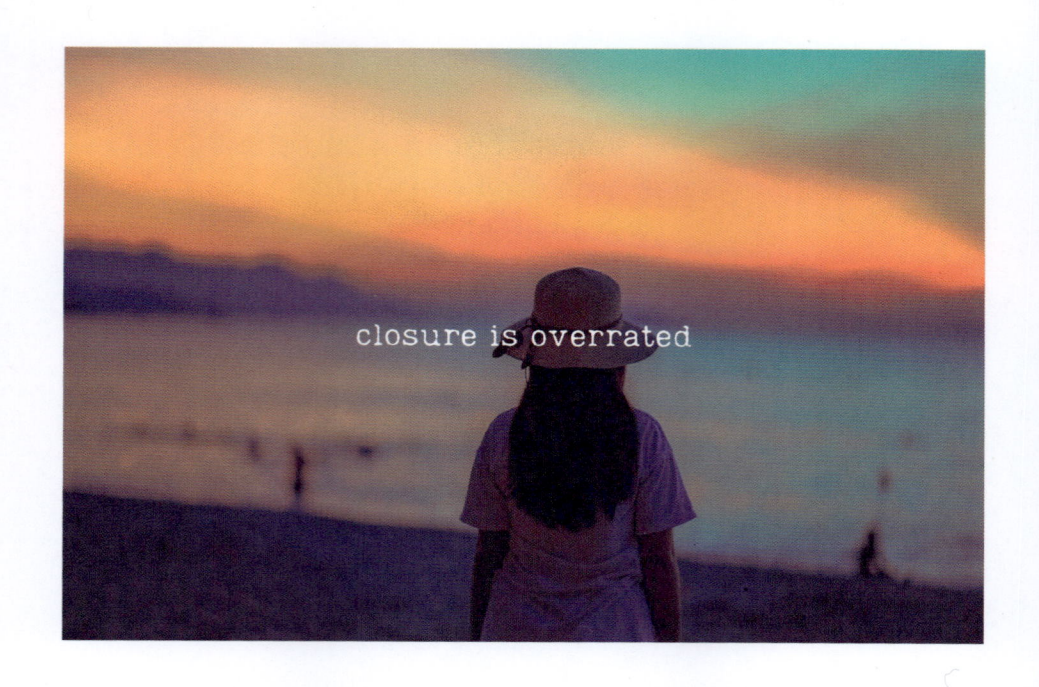

closure is overrated

the sunsets of my mind

l d stranack

sometimes we love people
like we love the stars,
we admire them from a distance
but never fail to be mesmerised
each time.

/LS

the sunsets of my mind

Printed in Poland
by Amazon Fulfillment
Poland Sp. z o.o., Wrocław